Writing: the drafting process

An examination of drafting in pupils' writing

Lorraine Dawes

NATE

Writing: the Drafting Process is published by the National Association for the Teaching of English (NATE), the UK subject teacher association for all aspects of the teaching of English from pre-school to university.

NATE
50 Broadfield Road
Broadfield Business Centre
Sheffield S8 0XJ
Tel: 0 114 255 5419
Fax: 0 114 255 5296

ISBN 0 901291 41 2

© NATE and author 1995

First published 1995

British Library Cataloguing in Publication Data. A catalogue record for this book is available from the British Library.

Apart from any fair dealing for the purposes of research or private study, or criticism or review, as permitted under the Copyright, Designs and Patents Act, 1988, this publication may only be reproduced, stored or transmitted, in any form or by any means, with the prior permission in writing of the publishers, or in the case of reprographic reproduction in accordance with the terms of licence issued by the Copyright Licensing Agency.

Cover design by Barry Perks Graphic Design
Printed in the United Kingdom by York Publishing Services, 64 Hallfield Road, Layerthorpe, York, Y03 7XQ

Contents

Foreword — iv

1 Introduction — 1
   Why draft? 1
   Making writing tasks explicit 1
   What form should drafting take? 2

2 Talk leading to writing — 6

3 Shared writing — 11

4 Drafting with pictures and diagrams — 15

5 Plans for supporting drafting — 18

6 Jigsaw drafting — 25

7 Responding to writing — 26

Appendixes — 30
   1 Books referred to in the text 30
   2 Story plan copymaster 31
   3 Example of a specific plan 32

Foreword

This booklet on the drafting process in writing offers suggestions for approaches to drafting. The ideas and examples are drawn from the whole primary age-range; the examples are of course from specific year-groups, but most of the suggestions can be used with a range of age-groups and with both fiction and non-fiction writing.

I thank the teachers and pupils in the London Borough of Redbridge with whom I have worked on developing the approaches in this booklet, especially the teachers from whose classes the examples are drawn: Sue Butcher, Catharine Dix, Sarah Evans, Jackie Gardner, Jenny Leach, Elaine Ross and Olive Thursby.

Lorraine Dawes

1 Introduction

Why draft?

Although there are many occasions when pupils and adults need to write 'straight off', this rarely happens without some preliminary thought. Most writing is drafted, whether it be in one's head, in diagrams or notes, or on a word processor. The significance of drafting varies with the intended audience – a letter to a close friend or relative can be drafted mentally, but an article for the well-informed readers of a professional magazine will need very thorough drafting and editing.

The National Curriculum recognises the importance of drafting in writing. Clear reference to it is made in the programmes of study: at Key Stage 1 in terms of 'opportunities to plan and review their writing' and very explicitly at Key Stage 2, where the stages of the writing process are identified.

Making writing tasks explicit

For pupils to feel in control of their own writing, they need to have clear expectations about the outcome. Teachers should give pupils as much information as possible about what is expected of their writing. All too often pupils are working in the dark when given a writing task:

Now I want you to write about it.

Imagine the thoughts that might run through the writer's head. Is this about real life, or is it fiction? Who is the writing for? Is it for public consumption, or just for me? What form should it take? Can I work with someone else? How long do I have to do it? Will it be for display? Will it be marked? What will she be looking for when she marks it? Should I be drafting it or writing it straight off? Have I seen an example of this sort of writing that I could use as a model for my own ideas?

Unfortunately, pupils don't ask themselves these questions (except maybe 'Can I work with someone else?'), and teachers don't always give them the information they need, which is perhaps why so many pieces of writing don't match up to expectations. Pupils are writing in the dark; it is the teacher's job to illuminate the task, or better still give them the means to illuminate it for themselves. To be fully informed, pupils need to know:

- the reason for the writing
- its purpose – what it should convey
- the form or genre to be used
- examples of similar writing that could provide a model
- an indication of length, perhaps in time terms
- what form drafting might take
- a suggestion about the proportion of time to be spent on drafting
- arrangements for getting feedback from others at draft stage
- availability of resources such as a dictionary, a thesaurus, writing materials
- the criteria for assessment.

If pupils are to assume responsibility for their writing, they need to develop an awareness of what they need to know before they start to write. Teachers need to be explicit when setting a writing task. Once pupils realise that this knowledge is important to their writing, they are in a position to make decisions for themselves. They need support while developing their independence, so writers should be offered first a limited choice, then a wider choice, then a free choice. For example, in the initial stages of encouraging a KS2 class to take responsibility for their writing, a teacher might say:

> *For this I want you to work with your writing partner, and write a newspaper story. Your writing will be used as a resource by Class 3 when they cover this topic next week, so it has to be clearly expressed, and presentation is important. You have the whole morning to draft it, but by 11.30 I want you to have joined up with another pair to listen to and improve each other's drafts. Don't forget our guidelines on talking about writing. You'll have half an hour during the week to make the final copy. You have read some similar newspaper stories, so bear those in mind when you are drafting, and refer to them for layout and style. The dictionaries and materials are in their usual place. When I read it I will be looking for the facts you include, and whether you have understood how people felt about what happened at the time. Any questions?*

This makes the task explicit. The next stage would be to offer a choice of, say, a letter or the transcript of a telephone conversation; later, a chart showing potential outcomes (as illustrated in the 'Plans' section; see page 22). As the pupils become more used to making their own decisions, the teacher can indicate the purpose and leave them to decide the most effective form for the writing.

Perhaps the pupils could be offered a checklist of what they need to think about before they write. It might look something like this:

Writing task
- What is it about?
- Do I work alone or with others?
- Why am I doing it?
- Who will read it?
- What form will it take – story, report, letter, diary entry, etc?
- What have I read that is similar and might give me a model to base it on?
- Where can I get ideas and help from?
- How long have I got?
- Whom do I discuss it with?
- What will my teacher be looking for when she reads it?

However they decide to support pupils' understanding of the task, one thing is very important: teachers themselves must have clear ideas about what the task involves, and how it fits in with their pupils' writing development.

What form should drafting take?

The National Curriculum

The Programme of Study for Key Stage 2 (Key skills) sets out the stages of the writing process:

Introduction

> *To develop their writing, pupils should be taught to:*
>
> - ***plan*** *– note and develop initial ideas;*
> - ***draft*** *– develop ideas from the plan into structured written text;*
> - ***revise*** *– alter and improve the draft;*
> - ***proofread*** *– check the draft for spelling and punctuation errors, omissions or repetitions;*
> - ***present*** *– prepare a neat, correct and clear final copy.*
>
> (KS2 Writing, para. 2b)

Planning

The planning stage should involve the writer in thinking and expressing ideas – probably in a hesitant and exploratory way. Having something in their hands can help very young pupils in this composing process – plasticine, playpeople, drawing materials.

Older pupils will want to note ideas down. Ask writers to brainstorm a list, make a web, draw a picture, fill in a plan, explain their intentions to another pupil or to the teacher; this is the initial planning stage and they should be aiming for good ideas. They need some idea of the time available for this initial stage. They should be encouraged to discuss their plans with a partner, if they are not already working in pairs. Pairs could ask another pair to act as response partners. Oral expression of ideas helps to create the language writers need to compose.

Drafting

Provide a drafting book or paper for drafting. Encourage writers to refer to their initial plans when writing. Emphasise that this is where they concentrate on the composition process; it is *what* they write that is important at this stage. Provide a thesaurus for improving composition. Again, give an indication of time.

This stage in the writing process is the best time for teacher intervention, because it is possible for the writer to act on suggestions and promptings. Once the presentation stage has been reached, it can be too late.

Revising

Revision can be done by the writer alone, but it may be more successful with a response partner. Once this practice is introduced, remind pupils to use response partners. Be explicit about considering content and expression. (Is it clear what you are saying in this writing? Is there a better way of saying it? Have you chosen the best order?) It is much easier just to pay attention to the presentation; remind them that attention to *content* and *expression* improves the writing most.

Reinforce this by modelling the process. Take a pupil's writing (with permission), read it out, celebrate the effective writing, and invite positive suggestions for improving the order, a particular phrase or sentence, etc. Ask the writer for his/her view of the suggestions. Share several pupils' writing during the same session, so no writer feels unfairly exposed.

This 'whole-class response partnership' can help to engender a cooperative ethos for writing; pupils enjoy feeling they are part of a community of writers, helping each other to become better writers.

Proofreading

Again, this may be better achieved in partnership than alone.

Presentation

Quality of presentation is greatly enhanced by having a real audience for the writing and by using models. Suggest to writers that they refer to similar texts to get presentational aspects right. For example, when writing dialogue, referring to a fiction book can help the writer punctuate direct speech correctly; when writing non-fiction, reference to an information book can help with headings and layout.

Drafting on the computer

Most of the samples in this document show pupils drafting in handwriting, but the computer is an excellent medium for drafting writing: it allows for correction, repositioning and other modifications without the whole text having to be written out again. The writer is in effect drafting right up to the moment 'print' is selected for the last time.

In a large class, it is not feasible for everyone to draft on the computer at any one time; but its use can be maximised by encouraging pupils to make a first draft on the computer, print it out and take it away to work on, then return later to make amendments and print out the final copy.

The National Curriculum makes clear reference to pupils planning, drafting and improving their writing 'on screen'.

Modelling the drafting process

Pupils need to be shown examples of the drafting process, so that they realise what it is and how useful it is, and so that they appreciate that it is something writers do in the real world. Teachers need to validate the drafting process by talking about it and providing examples for pupils to use as models for their own drafting. Authors invited to talk to pupils about their writing can provide insight into the drafting process by showing and talking about their latest book in all its stages – first ideas, early drafts, page proofs and final copy.

Showing a typical school letter home in all its stages – the headteacher's note that it needs to be written, what it is to include, rough draft, final typed copy – provides a very real example for pupils to read and discuss.

Pupils' plans, drafts and final versions can be displayed, rather than just showing final versions.

Pupils who are not familiar with drafting

Collaborative writing is a good 'way in' to the drafting process because drafting is necessary when two writers are working together to produce a piece of writing.

It is best to start with pairs, and to choose an activity that can be worked on together and then written about. A decision-making activity, an investigative maths or science activity, a story-telling or drama activity are all ideal.

Writing 'straight off'

It needs to be said that not every piece of writing requires drafting. Sometimes it is just not necessary. Also, there are many occasions where writers need to produce their best writing with minimal preparation. Teachers need to give opportunities for both kinds of writing situations, to teach pupils to write both with and without drafting, and to be able to decide when it is appropriate to draft and when it is not.

Similarly, not every piece of writing needs to go through the full five stages of the writing process. There may be some occasions where the process of composing is the learning objective, and there is little point in carrying it through to final copy.

Examples of the writing process

In the examples that follow of pupils' writing, several methods of drafting are included:

- talk leading to writing
- shared writing
- drafting with pictures and diagrams
- plans for supporting drafting
- jigsaw drafting
- responding to drafting.

2 Talk leading to writing

Pair talk

Talk is a necessary prerequisite for writing for young pupils. They need to put into words what they are thinking of writing. A class discussion following the reading of a story can give some pupils a chance to voice their thoughts, and give all the pupils a chance to hear language relevant to what they might want to write later, but every pupil still needs the opportunity to talk, in pairs or threes, about what they might write.

Infants in a reception/Y1 class shared the story *Who Sank the Boat?* by Pamela Allen, and afterwards talked to each other about writing to Mr Peffer to tell him who did sink his boat.

Angelee read her letter aloud (see below):

> *Dear Mr Peffer, your boat is broken because all the animals broke it. Cow, donkey. Please write back.*

Her invented spellings show the beginnings of knowledge of how letters represent sounds, easily seen in the 'P R bc' for 'Please write back'. Talking about what is being written helps the recognition of sounds, and also the composition of the message itself.

Charlotte read her letter:

> *Dear Mr Peffer, the cow went in, the donkey, the pig got in, the sheep, the mouse got in. love Charlotte.*

Angelee

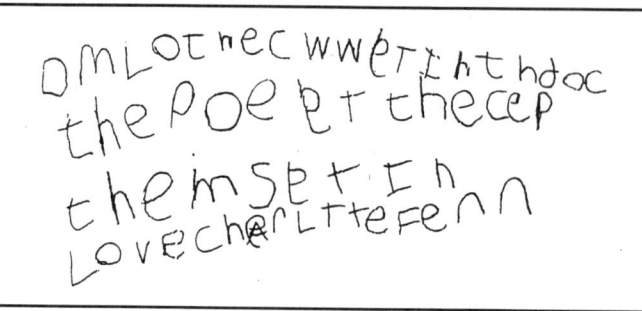

Charlotte

Talk leading to writing

Pupils composing at the computer need the opportunity to talk aloud about their writing. These infant pupils were able to appreciate the need for the use of the third person in a newspaper by talking about who might read it.

> **OUR NEWSPAPLE**
>
> WE HAVMADE 24 FUNY FACES.
> Davinder made funny face with lots of noses.
> niraj made a face with glasses.

In the following example of factual writing, Y2 pupils had made a book about their visit to Mountfitchet Castle. They talked about what they liked best to their partner before they wrote. Holding a pretend microphone, they asked each other, 'What did *you* like best about Mountfitchet Castle?' Such oral drafting can help young writers retain the thread of their composition while they are occupied in the mechanics of writing it down.

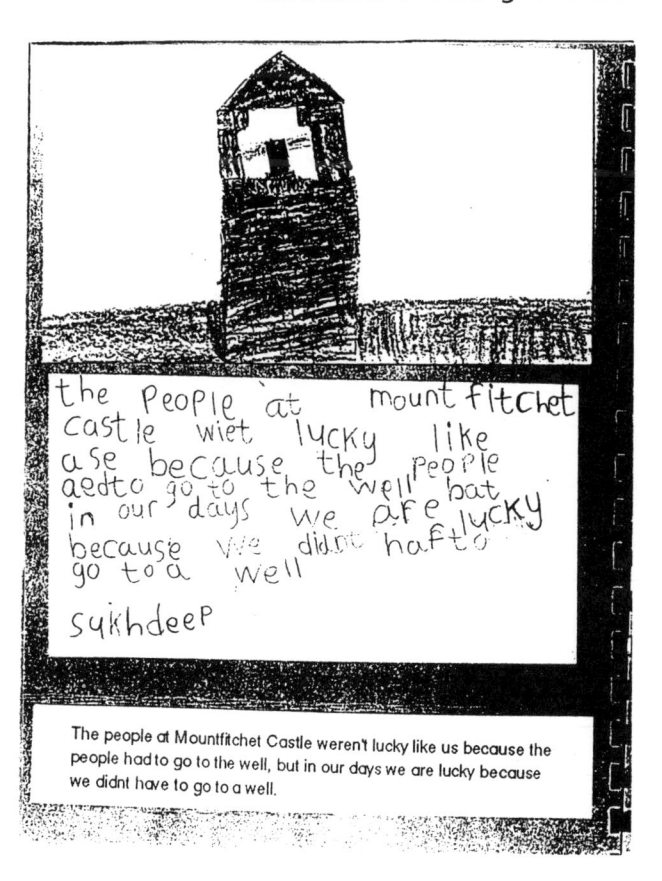

Sukhdeep's writing took a long time to get down on paper, but he knew exactly what he wanted to tell the reader.

Each writer read his or her writing aloud to the teacher, who typed it and printed it out. This was stuck at the bottom of the page, so the book could be used as a reading resource by other pupils. This is useful when you want the writing to be easily read, but don't wish to 'correct' pupils' own efforts; pupils readily agree to a transcription in 'book writing'.

> the People at mount fitchet Castle wiet lucky like use because the people aedto go to the well bat in our days we are lucky because we didnt hafto go to a well
>
> sukhdeep

> The people at Mountfitchet Castle weren't lucky like us because the people had to go to the well, but in our days we are lucky because we didnt have to go to a well.

Writing: the Drafting Process

Interviewing

Writing news is often more useful if pupils interview each other about what they did and write their partner's news rather than their own. It helps the writer to select the most important things to write about.

This example, a rough draft, contains many facts which reflect both the writer's and David's priorities. This draft was not edited further or written up; its value was in the process of questioning, listening and reporting. Neither pupils nor teachers should feel that every piece of writing needs to be worked on. There are plenty of occasions when it is best left after the first attempt. Pupils can very easily be put off writing by the thought that everything will need to be copied out again. If it had been decided to develop this further, the writer could have read it to a response partner to gain feedback, modified the writing as necessary and collaborated with others on her table to produce a newsletter.

> davids half tirme Hollday
> David went to London
> for his half term
> Holiday he said it was
> boring. He went on
> Tuesday he took a
> paked lunch with him
> in the paked
> lunch he had bread
> and biscuits and crisps
> and a drink and he
> hot lots of books
> and it was davids
> birthday on monday

Interviewing

'Telephoning'

When pupils are writing about facts and opinions, oral drafting can often be made easier by role-play using the telephone. Somehow it is easier to select the important things you want to say when you are talking to someone a long way away!

Some Y5 pupils had been studying the plague, and had listened to an account of life in the plague village of Eyam. In pairs, they role-played being a villager telephoning a friend or relative far away to warn them about the plague. They appreciated that, at the time, this would have been an impossibility but were still able to think themselves back in time while pretending to hold a telephone. The conversations they held with each other enabled them to rehearse what would be later written in a letter – much more appropriate to the period.

Mhairi has conveyed a sense of the times by her choice of language. The account of Eyam had many contemporary quotations in it, and she probably used these as a model for her own writing.

Eyam

Dear Kerry (My sister),

Hope you are well. Bad news, the Plague has reached Eyam. The family are dead and only I remain. Sadly I have caught the Plague and I fear I shall die. I have seen a doctor and he told me I had the Plague. When you write back I fear I shall not be alive to read it so I better say goodbye now but before I do I wish to say that Peter still lives without infection. A lady will take him to you. Look after him well.

love

Mhairi

Directions

Some Y5/Y6 pupils, writing out directions from a map, spent a long time talking it through with their partners, writing the directions in rough, and reading them back to each other to check before making the final copy. Their audience was clear: other pupils would attempt to find the destination by following the directions. Their early discussion was exploratory:

> *You pass that road, you pass this road.*
>
> *No, you go up that road . . . Is this called Eastern Avenue?*
>
> *Yeah, E . . . A . . . S . . . T . . . E . . . R . . . N.*

but by the final copy they had switched to the standard imperative form:

> **Directions.**
>
> Turn right at the school gate.
> Turn right after about $\frac{1}{8}$ of a mile into Aldborough Road South. Walk down Aldborough Road South.
> Turn right after about $\frac{1}{4}$ of a mile into Wands Road.
> Turn right at Glebelands Ave.
> Walk for about $\frac{1}{4}$ of a mile.
> Cross Eastern Avenue.
> You have reached your destination.

The role of talk in composing should not be underestimated. It is well worth planning a time for role-play, interviewing or discussion if pupils are to produce writing of quality. The activity needs to be structured if talk is not to slide off the point; so set a specific task, decide on groupings, explain the reason behind the activity, give some idea of time. Afterwards, when the pupils share their writing, they might reflect on the effect talking had on their writing.

3 Shared writing

Shared writing, where pupils compose together while their teacher scribes, is extremely valuable for modelling the writing process. How do very young pupils find out what writing is? By seeing writers write and read what they have written. Often, in their early days at school, they gain a concept of what school writing is by watching other pupils write.

Teachers can make this learning easier and more explicit by going through the writing process with them every day. If the teacher is the scribe, the mechanics of writing are removed; the pupils compose, see their words appear, and read them back. They see the purpose in writing, and feel the satisfaction of being a writer.

In these examples, young pupils are jointly composing writing that will become part of their reading resources.

Instant books

Some reception/Y1 pupils listened to the story *Donkey's Dreadful Day* by Irina Hale, about a donkey who is allowed to serve all the circus animals with their food, but gets everything mixed up. With the teacher scribing on a large sheet of paper pinned to an easel, the pupils recalled what the animals liked to eat, and their own favourite foods:

Elephants like to eat hay but Rashel likes ice-cream.

Sea-lions like to eat fish but Viresh likes pizza.

The pupils helped with decisions about where to start writing on the paper, what letters might be needed, how to spell names, etc. – it is surprising how much help a teacher needs in a shared writing situation! Then the pupils chose an animal each, and made two pages of a book, using the same format. The pages were stuck into a book and the text written along the bottom of each page. The book was shared with everyone at the end of the session.

Dogs like to eat bones

but Sofiya likes spaghetti

Writing: the Drafting Process

A Y1 class made a book in a similar way as a follow-up to reading *Bear Hunt* by Anthony Browne. In this story Bear has a magic pencil with which he draws his way out of trouble. The shared writing stage provided a model for the pupils' writing.

If I was hyngry I would draw dinner

Individual books

After listening to *Don't Forget the Bacon* by Pat Hutchins, pupils talked about going shopping. With the teacher scribing on a large sheet of paper, they jointly composed some 'rules' about going shopping:

Shopping

be careful so you don't get lost
take a shopping list
take a basket or bag
take some money
Wait for your change
Don't forget what you bought
Stop when a car is coming

Shared writing

Each pupil then made a little book of their own about going shopping. Here are two pages from Adrian's book:

Group book

Sharing *Goodnight Owl* by Pat Hutchins led to a discussion of what keeps us awake, and a retelling of the story with one of the pupils as the main character. The story was written up as it was composed, with the repetition of *'and Devinder tried to sleep'* after every new idea. When a group of pupils made their own book, the model for their writing was there for them to refer to.

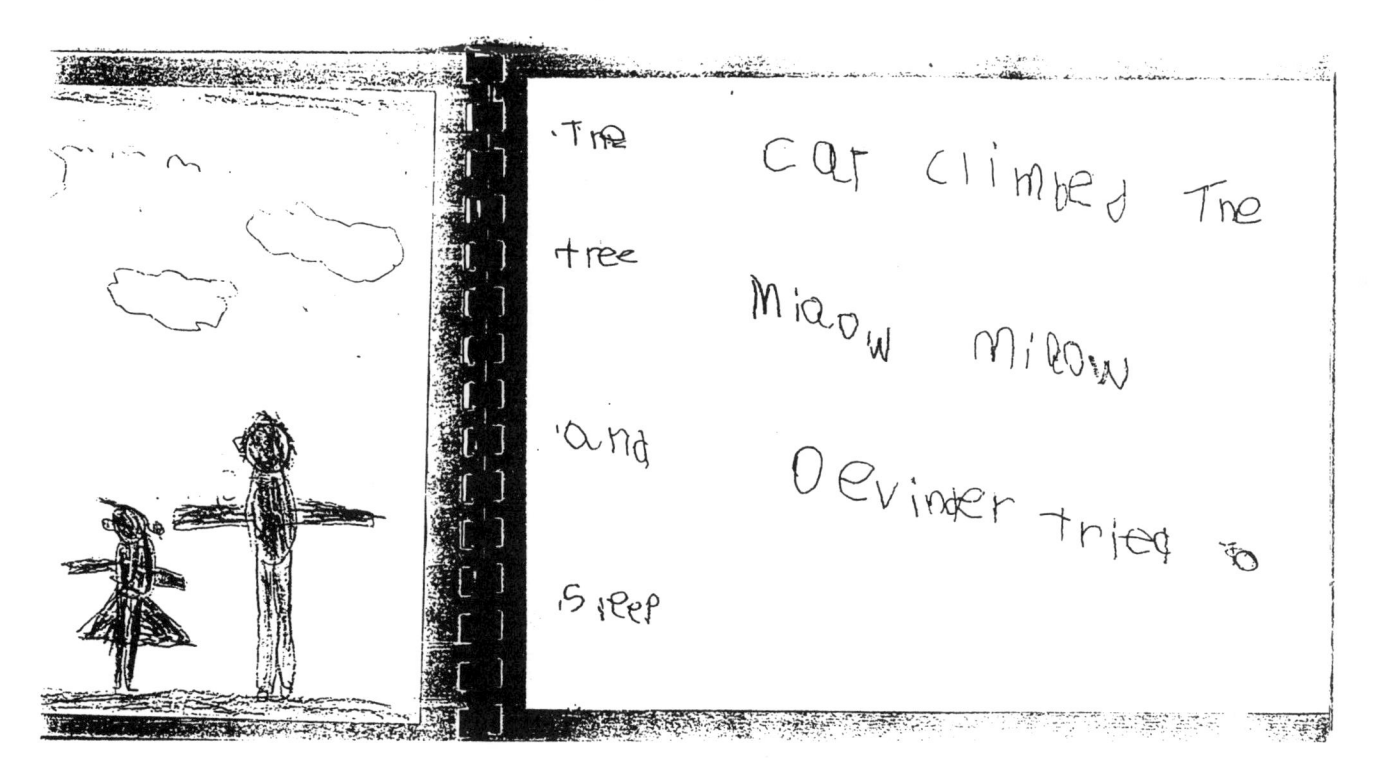

Shared writing provides a model of drafting that pupils can readily grasp. It allows pupils to understand the pleasure of being a writer and learn about the writing process. It is a complete activity, comprising talking, composing, reading, altering, re-reading and enjoying. The purpose and audience are clear, and it provides an accessible model for pupils' individual writing.

Shared writing is not only for young pupils. Teachers of older pupils will recognise how often the process of reporting back group work results in collaborative drafting on the blackboard. It can, for example, be a useful way of enabling pupils to compose the most succinct way of expressing a sentence. The experience of shared writing leads easily on to collaborative drafting, where a group negotiates the most effective way of expressing what they want to write.

4 Drafting with pictures and diagrams

Sequencing pictures

Pictures photocopied or drawn from a story provide an excellent resource to support oral drafting when pupils are retelling stories. Pairs can be given a set of six pictures of significant scenes in the story and asked to put them in the correct order and then to take it in turns to tell each other the story. Discussion about the sequence starts the pupils using the vocabulary and structures of the story so that, when they reach the more formal task of telling each other the story, the language is already there in their heads. Sometimes pupils are reluctant to do the retelling – they would rather proceed directly to writing their version – but it is an important stage in the drafting. It helps the pupils feel the writer's 'voice'; it ensures the story makes sense; it helps them develop more detail; it reinforces the idea of narrative structure.

Six pictures fit onto a sheet of A4 whilst remaining a reasonable size. They can be drawn or reduced on a photocopier. After retelling the story in pairs, pupils can be given extra sheets of pictures to enable every pupil to write their own story. Concertina books made of coloured paper for the pupils to stick the pictures in are easy to make and attractive, but it is advisable to provide white paper on which to write the text.

Here are two examples of the end of the story *There's Something Spooky in my Attic,* from the same Y3/Y4 class – one by an experienced writer, and the other by a beginner in English. For both pupils, the retelling of this story has been a complete and worthwhile activity, resulting in a book they can read to others with a sense of achievement.

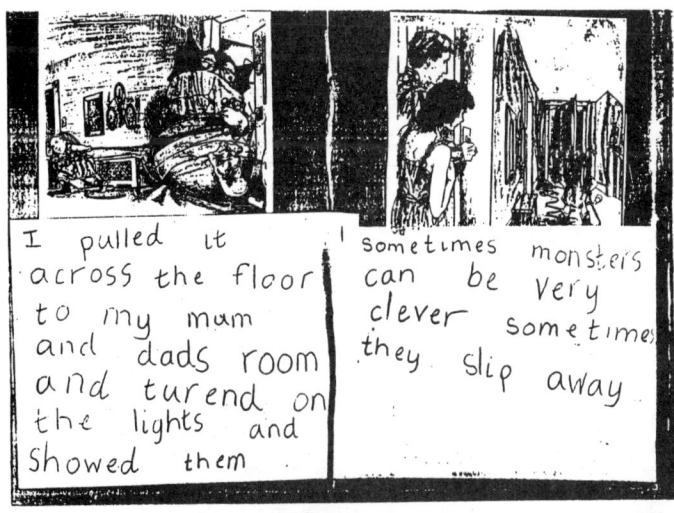

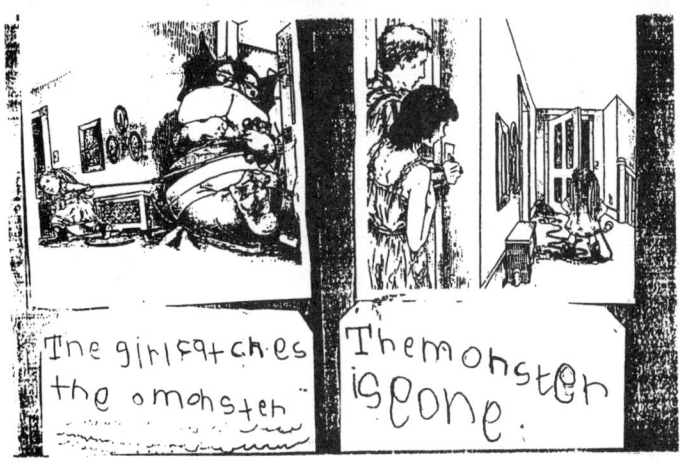

I pulled it across the floor to my mum and dads room and turend on the lights and showed them

Sometimes monsters can be very clever sometimes they slip away

The girl fatches the o monster

The monster is gone.

Writing: the Drafting Process

Deciding a layout

A Y5/Y6 class were placed in groups and given the task of planning a park. Assuming the role of a leisure business, they had to present a written report to the Council with their proposals for the park. Each group had a plan of the park and areas to fit into it, and a list of factors to take into account.

As the groups made decisions about the layout of the park, they were rehearsing the language that they would be using in their report, full of explanations and reasons:

> *There's nothing around it – if we put it in the trees it might look better.*
>
> *Skateboarding could be here, then.*
>
> *No, that's outside the park, isn't it?*
>
> *No, here's the park wall.*
>
> *It's too near – it would be dangerous. Put it here . . .*
>
> *No, it's too cramped. Up by the Over 7s playground . . .*

Having decided on a layout, the groups then drafted their report collaboratively. The discussion over the plan ensured that they all were involved and had something to offer. The finished reports contained the reasoning that had been expressed in the oral discussions.

> **Council Report**
>
> We have placed one of the toilets outside the park so when the park is closed people could still use the toilet. We have also placed the games pitch near the entrance so that if it starts raining it would be quicker for people to go out. We have put the skate boarding area near the over 7's playground so that kids can get out of the over 7's playground and just take one foot step and they will be there. We placed the paddling pool next to the under sevens playground because little children like to splash about alot. We have put the pond near the rose border so that the public can look around at our garden. We have placed a shelter near the games pitch so that when people have been playing a long game and when it finished they can rest there. The bin is next to the shelter so that people can throw their rubbish in the bin. We have put a sandpit next to the under sevens playground for them to play with. That is our park report.
>
> By Harminder, Sukhdeep and Sukhbir

Decision-making is made easier by having a diagram or plan to focus on (people often seem able to think better when they have something in their hands), and the interplay of ideas as decisions are made is a useful prelude to the interplay of ideas as writing is drafted.

Drafting with pictures and diagrams

Making suggestions, accepting, rejecting, modifying, offering alternatives, justifying, agreeing, reaching a consensus – these are all behaviours that come fairly easily in oral decision-making.

Collaborative drafting is potentially more fraught, there is more at stake when things are written down. But it is possible to carry on the easy discussion, the interplay of ideas, the search for the best solution into the drafting process if there has been a fruitful period of oral decision-making first.

Illustration as drafting

Drawing is a useful support to discussion and composing, and should be considered as another form of drafting. It is most effective when two pupils are drawing one picture together, and talking about it as they draw. Their description of the picture is likely to be very detailed and fluent because they will have been giving each other a running commentary as they drew.

Following a reading of *The Cat with Two Tales*, by Nathan and Hedley, a Y1 class talked about what would happen if a cat visited their classroom. They thought of all the places in the room and the things that went on during the day that the cat might be interested in.

Each pair of pupils was given one situation to draw, for example playtime, the book corner, PE. As they drew they inevitably told each other about what was happening in their picture so that, when the teacher went round asking questions and making notes, the descriptions were detailed and fluent. The pupils' pictures were put in a book, and their ideas used to provide a narrative that involved all the pupils, and told the story of *The Cat that Came to School*.

Such books are bound to provide popular reading resources for early readers because they can recognise their own words in the narrative as well as their own drawings and names.

> Neil and Philip were by the drinking fountain. Tiger came along to have a drink. Neil lifted her up and Philip pulled the handle back.
>
> Adam and Ryan were in the book corner. Tiger chose a book and saw a snake, so she ate the book up. Ryan and Adam hid the books with mice in, so she didn't eat them!
>
> Tiger was eating cat food at dinner time in the hall. Emily and Eimear helped her with her bowl. Tiger got fatter and fatter!

5 Plans for supporting drafting

Story plans

Story plans are a useful way of focusing pupils' attention on the composition of a story, especially when they are working together to compose. The prompts at the bottom of a plan support the writers' discussion and composition. Infants, having made 'passports' as part of their topic, collaborated in pairs on a story of a journey. They chose where to go and planned their story using this simple story plan:

STORY PLAN by Shama and Aamina

We want to go to Mombasa Africa	We went in an aeroplane	We saw Aamina's Mummy. We all held hands.	Then we come home
Where do you want to go?	How do you get there?	What did you do? Who do you see?	How does your story end?

Then each pupil made a little book, following the plan but elaborating on the illustrations. They each decided on a title, and drew an illustration of themselves as author on the back. The teacher interviewed each author and wrote a biographical comment, just as real books often have.

I went to Mombasa by Shama
(FRONT PAGE)

We went to Mombasa

Cont'd

Plans for supporting drafting

> We went in an aeroplane
>
> We saw Aamina's mummy we all held hands
>
> Then we came home
>
> Shama is six years old and she wrote this story with Aamina.
>
> (BACK PAGE)

A Y3/Y4 class, who had retold and written their own version of many stories, used a similar story plan to create personal stories. They chose to work individually or in pairs. In this case the prompts at the bottom of the plan needed to be more general, but they still supported the shape of the story. Writers could use extra sheets if they needed more space for the middle of their story.

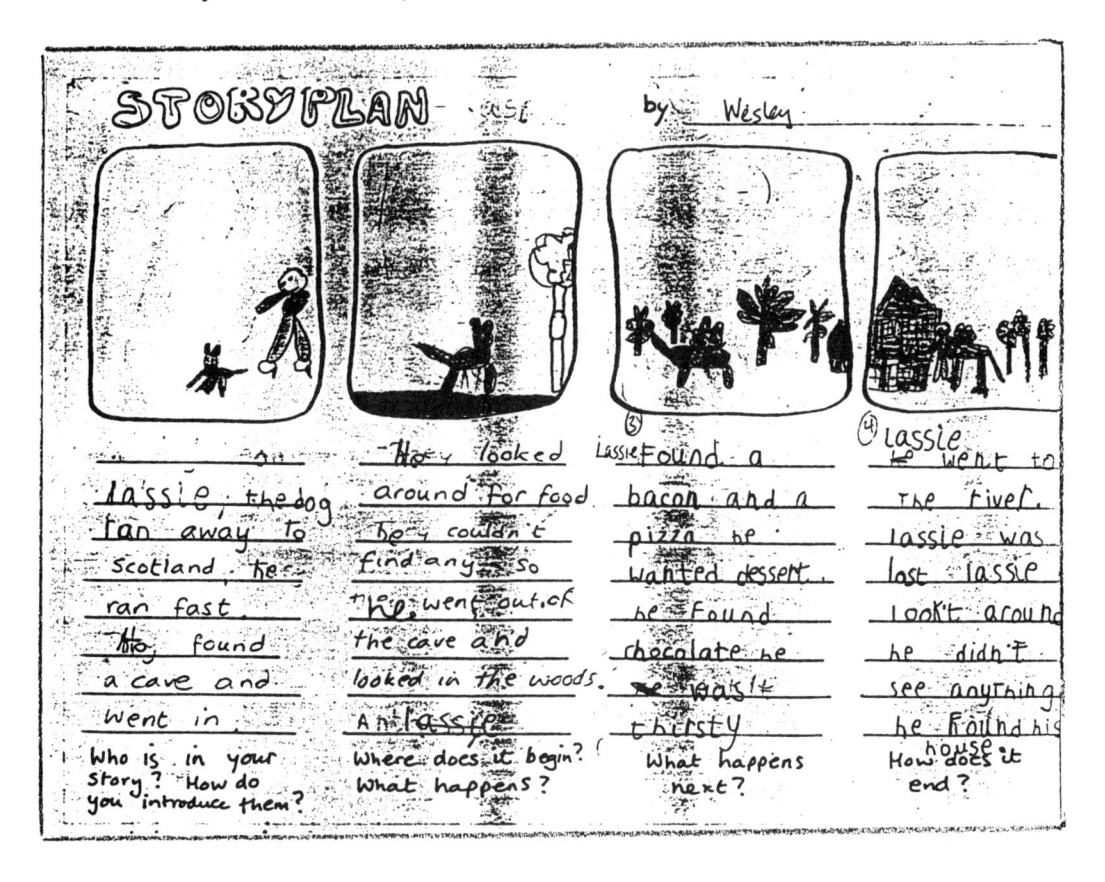

> STORY PLAN by Wesley
>
> (1) Lassie the dog ran away to Scotland he ran fast he found a cave and went in.
>
> (2) They looked around for food they couldn't find any so he went out of the cave and looked in the woods. An lassie
>
> (3) Lassie found a bacon and a pizza he wanted dessert he found chocolate he was thirsty
>
> (4) Lassie he went to the river. lassie was lost lassie look't around he didn't see anything he found his house
>
> 1. Who is in your story? How do you introduce them?
> Where does it begin? What happens?
> What happens next?
> How does it end?

19

Writing: the Drafting Process

Writers, having drafted on the story plan, read their stories to other pupils to obtain feedback, before making alterations. A final check on spelling and punctuation was made by the teacher because these stories would have a real audience. Each part of the story was copied onto card, as were the illustrations, and the set of cards jumbled up. Other pupils read the cards and sequenced the story.

These pupils had the opportunity to reflect on how they felt their writing was going after nearly a term of sequencing and retelling, writing own versions of stories, and writing their own stories. Their comments showed a real sense of progress and satisfaction:

My writing's a lot better now.

I thought this story was very nice when I planned it . . . I'm very pleased with the pictures.

You have to think about forming letters properly because someone's going to read it.

Now I can write stories better myself.

Plans for supporting drafting

Specific plans

The story plan (a blank version is provided in Appendix 2) can be modified to suit many purposes, but often it is useful to design a specific plan to support a particular piece of writing.

In this example, groups of Y5/Y6 pupils were hypothesising about how the invention of the wheel had occurred and the plan was designed to support their thinking and discussion. A further (blank) example of a specific plan is provided in Appendix 3.

The invention of the Wheel

In your group, make up a story together about the invention of the first wheel. Jot down notes when you have come to an agreement about how it happened.

How did the first wheel come to be invented?
Thousounds and thousounds of years ago an architect was sitting in his invention chair and came up with the idea of having a wheel on his paper he came up with a round shape figure what was going to be made out of wood. He made it and tried it out then some one decovered it one night

Who was involved?
An architect called John B. Dunlop

What did it look like?
It was a round shape figure that was made out of wood

What was it made of - how was it actually made?
It was made out of a peace of a tree trunk carver and an axe.
It was made by chopping up a peace wood from a tree trunk and using a carver it was smoothed up and then it had holes cut in the middle.

Groups could decide how they wished to present their story and the chart showed what kinds of drafting they would need for each outcome. Writers have greater control over their writing if they can decide on the form of the final outcome, but simply saying 'Choose how you want to do it' can give the impression that the outcome doesn't matter. Offering the options in a structured way helps pupils realise that their decisions are important and have implications for how they will work. It gives status and purpose to the drafting process.

Invention of the wheel – Options		
	DRAFT FORMS	OUTCOME
Story	telling, writing	tape / written
Play	acting, writing	tape / performance
Inventor's account – letter	talk, writing	letter
Conversation	talk, writing	tape / written
diary	writing	diary extract
News report	talk, writing, computer	Newspaper article
Instructions	talk, writing	tape / written instructions

There were a range of outcomes in the class which helped to promote pupils' interest in the work of other groups, and a general broadening of expectations about writing. If teachers want to lift pupils out of the rut of writing in rough books, then copying out neatly, a range of writing experiences needs to be offered and the responsibility for the form of the writing placed in the hands of the writer. Pupils need to be able to draft with the purpose and audience in mind – as writers do in the real world.

Here is the transcript of two attempts at a radio newsflash by a member of the group who wrote the plan shown above. Interestingly, she chose an option that was not explicitly suggested on the chart. She drafted in writing, but modified the work during her taping attempts in order to include more of the pop radio genre.

```
First attempt

"A new architect has just invented the most....ahem...popular
thing that probably will be in generations. It is called the
wheel. It works round and round. It could be useful to us.
It...He could make it into something else, we don't know yet, what
yet, but it is a mystery. At home he is working and he is trying
to make something out of it.
He...It is made out of wood and it go- rolls round and round.
We can use it if he ...we can use it (excuse me for that)if he
can come up with a new invention and then it will be the most
probably popular thing in the world, and it will be popular for
generations and generations.
We only have the latest yet, tune into us at Capital FM."

Second attempt

"Today an architect has invented a new invention. It is called
the wheel. It works....it works...right, it works like when you
roll it it works round and round. It is made out of wood and
it...it is cut from a tree-trunk.
We have just heard that his friend... friend in his back yard. He
asked him what it was. It was like I told you earlier, something
that goes round and round and is...can be useful to us. At the
moment he is at home working himself to the bone making more and
more.
We only have the latest - tune into us, Radio Flash, on Capital
FM 101."
```

Plans for supporting drafting

Plans for poems

This plan is to support the writing of a poem, after pupils have heard and read a few examples of similar poems. It enables pupils to utilise what they have learned from reading other poems without those poems interfering too much in their own compositions. The format provides a framework to support their own ideas.

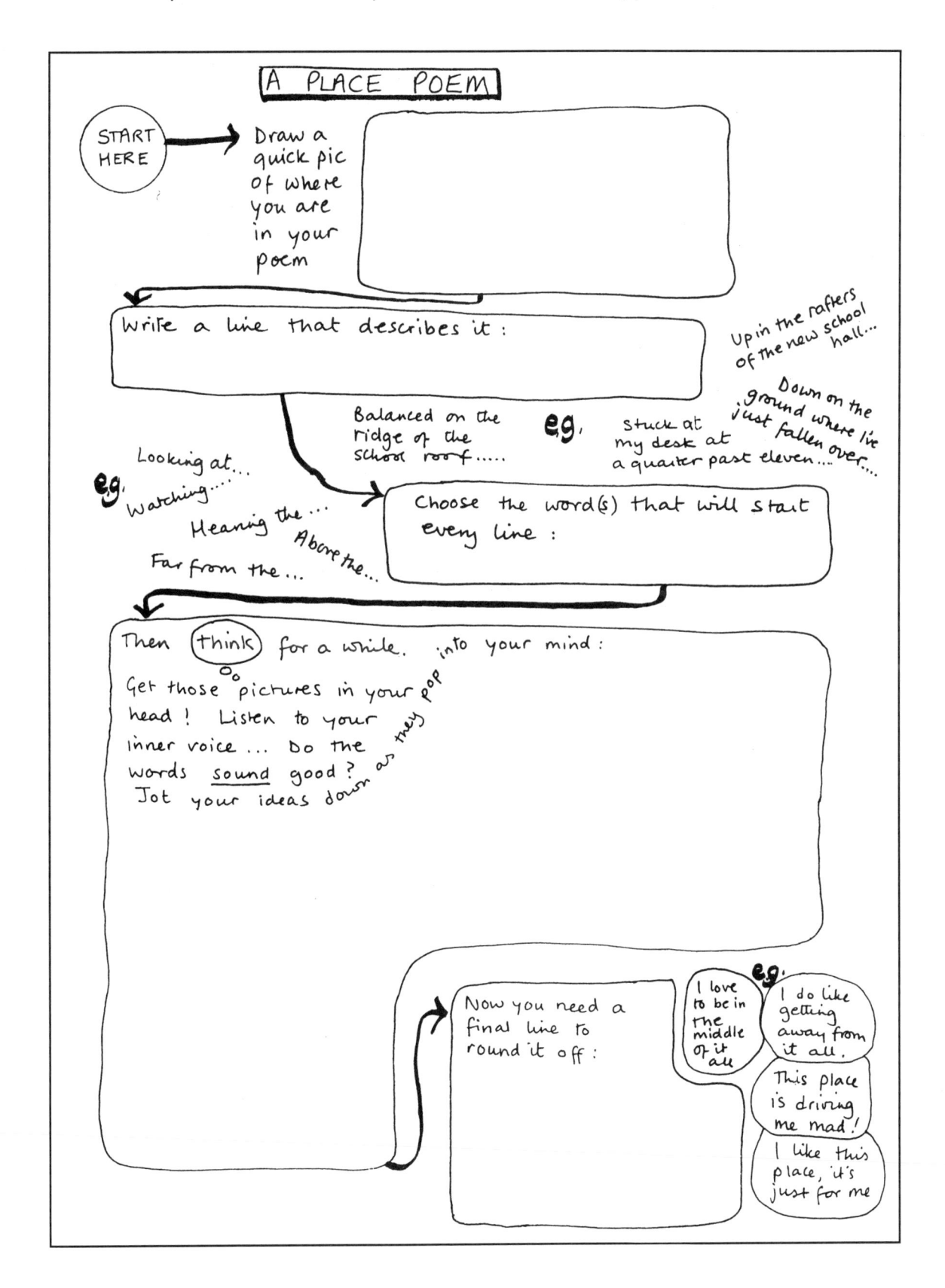

A PLACE POEM

START HERE → Draw a quick pic of where you are in your poem

Write a line that describes it:

eg. Balanced on the ridge of the school roof...... Stuck at my desk at a quarter past eleven.... Up in the rafters of the new school hall... Down on the ground where I've just fallen over...

eg. Looking at... Watching.... Hearing the... Above the... Far from the...

Choose the word(s) that will start every line:

Then (think) for a while. Get those pictures in your head! Listen to your inner voice... Do the words *sound* good? Pop into your mind: Jot your ideas down as they pop

Now you need a final line to round it off:

eg. I love to be in the middle of it all. I do like getting away from it all. This place is driving me mad! I like this place, it's just for me

---

23

The value of plans

Plans are an effective way to support pupils' drafting of writing. They can:

- provide a framework for thought
- indicate the directions in which the writing might move
- suggest examples of words or structures which can set the writer off on the right track
- keep the writer to the point
- ensure the writer perceives planning as a valuable – and valued – stage in writing
- enable response partners to quickly understand what the writer is trying to do
- facilitate modifications and improvements at a useful stage in the writing process
- focus discussion when writers collaborate.

Because the plan looks and feels different to a prose draft, there is not that sense of 'having to write it out again' when the final version is written.

When designing a plan for writers to use, try to break the composing process down into stages. Choose appropriately-sized spaces for writing or drawing in. Include clear instructions and, if necessary, some suggested words or pictures to stimulate thinking. Make it look attractive.

When you offer it to the pupils, emphasise that it is a plan to work on. They can change and improve the ideas as they use it, and they should talk it over with others. Give them an indication of the time available for drafting, and a deadline for the final outcome, so that they understand what is expected.

6 Jigsaw drafting

Jigsaw drafting is useful when the writing task needs sharing out yet every pupil needs to be involved in the final outcome. It is best described by an example.

A Y5/Y6 class went on a visit to the Museum of Transport, and found out about buses. In home groups of six, they decided which two would write about horse buses, which two would write about early motor buses, and which two would write about later motor buses. Then all the home groups split up and re-formed into three specialist groups: one focusing on horse buses, one on early motor buses, and one on later motor buses.

In the specialist groups, the pupils brainstormed all they could remember about their particular type of bus, and wrote about it on a big sheet of paper. They read it back and thought about the best order. Then, each pair drafted the writing they wanted to take back to their home group.

Each pair read out their draft to the rest of the specialist group, and listened to other pairs' drafts. They made improvements until they had the writing as they wanted it, and were ready to go back to the home groups.

Back in the home group, each pair read out their draft to the others. Everyone got to hear what each member of the home group had written about either horse buses, early motor buses or late motor buses. Together they planned how to present all the information, and produced the finished writing in the form of a detailed poster which other classes could read.

Part of an early draft in the 'specialist group'

Another class used this method for producing books of their visit to the British Museum. After a whole-class discussion reviewing what they had learned about and deciding on specialist group topics, each home group took responsibility for allocating members to specialist groups, sharing and improving the drafts they brought back, and editing and producing the final book. The books were on display at the parents' evening, together with a poster with photographs explaining the processes that led to the final outcome. It is important to value the process as well as the outcome.

The advantages of jigsaw drafting are clear, especially for writing about something like a school visit. It enables the pupils to focus on the educational content of the visit, rather than the journey and the lunch; the writing-up task is enjoyable, not daunting; pupils have the opportunity to pool their recollections; there is the sense of a community of writers working together to produce the best possible account and the end product can be a polished piece of writing that is accessible to its audience.

7 Responding to drafting

Guidelines for talking about writing with a partner

An integral part of the drafting process is trying out one's draft on a potential reader. This person needs to respond to the writing in a constructive way if the interchange is to be of any use to the writer. So it is well worthwhile spending time helping pupils consider how to respond to writing.

One way of doing this is to pose the question 'What makes writing *good*?' As the class respond, write all their comments on a flip chart or blackboard, sorting them into two categories as you do so. Write all comments relating to the composing process on the left side, and those relating to the mechanical aspects of writing on the right. (This positioning is to reflect the order in which these aspects need to be addressed: content first, then presentation.) You may need to ask more questions to elicit the responses you have in mind, but always use the pupils' own words.

Then, ask the class to think silently for a minute or two about why you have sorted their comments in this way. With younger pupils, you may need to give them some clues: the analogy of an author with a secretary will help. Which person is responsible for which category? The pupils can reflect on which person is most important in making the book a successful book, and through this come to realise that the composing process is the most important part of writing.

Pupils, of course, are both author and secretary, so they will have to pay attention to both categories. But, as the National Curriculum points out, it makes more sense to concentrate on composition first, and presentation later. 'Revise' comes before 'proofread'.

It is worth stressing that when a writer shares her or his writing with a partner, it should be read aloud first, so as to give the partner a chance to concentrate on the composition. Reading aloud removes the whole area of spelling and punctuation from consideration. The response partner will then find it easier to concentrate on content and expression as they look at the writing together. When the *content* is satisfactory, the secretarial details can be dealt with.

The class's comments can be edited into guidelines for talking about writing with a partner. Displayed as a poster, or photocopied onto A5 card, it will provide a reference point for pairs of pupils working on their writing.

Shown opposite is one example of guidelines for talking about writing with a partner that was developed by a Y5 class.

Helping pupils to become good response partners

Pupils should be encouraged to recognise the importance of a positive and sympathetic attitude when responding to another person's writing. This can be done through role-playing good and bad response partners. (It is helpful to introduce both terms, *response partner* and *writing partner*, and see which the pupils prefer to use.)

Each pupil needs to have an early draft of a piece of writing, preferably with a clear audience and purpose, which they have not discussed before. (You could set a writing task for this purpose, e.g. a letter to their parents describing the range of writing they have done recently; what kind of writing task they like best/find most difficult; what writing instrument and paper they prefer, etc.) Explain that they are going to do some role-play to explore what is most helpful in discussing writing.

Talking about writing with a partner

Ask your partner to read his or her writing aloud to you.
Listen carefully.
Then read it yourself.

Is it good to read?

1. Is the writing interesting / enjoyable / informative?
   Point out to your partner a line or two that you think is good.

2. Is there anything that is not clear?
   Talk about it and discuss how it could be better put.

3. Is there enough detail?
   Can you suggest any helpful words or expressions?

Is it easy to read?

1. Do any spellings need checking?
   Underline any spellings you are not sure of, and use a dictionary to help you check them.

2. Are all the capital letters and full stops in the right places?
   Pencil in any improvements.

Now do the same with your own writing – read it to your partner and listen to her or his ideas.

After your discussions you should be in a good position to improve your writing. Read it through and think about the changes you want to make, then write your improved version. Show it to your partner and say thank you for her or his help.

Writing: the Drafting Process

1. With pupils in pairs, ask them to decide who will be 'A' and who will be 'B'.

2. Ask the 'A's to read their writing aloud to the 'B's, then discuss it. The 'B's must role-play being really bad response partners. If you take photographs, these can be used to make a poster. Stop after a short time, once you think they have got the idea.

3. Ask the 'B's what they did to show they were being a bad response partner. Write these descriptions up on the blackboard under the title 'Bad response partners . . .'

4. Swap roles, so the 'A's are being bad response partners. Take more photographs, as the body language will be very explicit now.

5. Now everyone has had experience of both roles, ask them how they felt as a writer with a bad response partner. Write these comments up under the heading, 'and the writer feels . . .'

6. Ask the 'B's to carry on sharing their writing with the 'A's, who will now role-play being really excellent response partners. Take photographs as before.

7. Discuss how they behaved to show they were good response partners, and write up under the heading, 'Good response partners . . .'

8. Swap and repeat as before, then discuss how the writer feels sharing writing with a good response partner. Write up under the heading 'and the writer feels . . .'

9. Read through the comments on the blackboard and reflect on how one's behaviour as a response partner can influence how the writer feels. Ask pupils to reflect on the kind of response partner they would like to share their writing with.

Older pupils can appreciate how writing is part of one's identity, and how unsympathetic criticism can affect one's self-esteem. Younger pupils tend to express this in terms of being 'kind' or 'wanting to be your friend' but the understanding is there, made explicit by the feelings engendered by the role-play.

The comments made by the pupils and the photographs can be used to make an effective poster to remind pupils about being good response partners in writing. An example of the text of such a poster is shown opposite.

Responding to writing

WRITING PARTNERS

Writers often need to discuss their writing with a partner.

Bad Writing Partners...

...are rude about the writing
...just cross out mistakes
...look at or do something else
...pretend to read it but ignore it really
...say 'Hold on a minute...'

and the writer feels...

...angry, mad, like beating him up
...that writing it was a waste of time
...it was embarrassing
...not very nice

Good Writing Partners...

...make agreeable noises as they read
...point out something that is good
...say nice things
...are helpful
...are kind and friendly
...have a nice manner of speaking
...are encouraging

and the writer feels...

...happy
...honoured, because they say it is nice
...more confident, because they are sensible
...it gives you more experience about writing

Sometimes it can be embarrassing to read or show your writing to someone else. Having a sympathetic writing partner really helps.

Appendix 1: Books referred to in the text

Allen, Pamela (1982) *Who Sank the Boat?* Hamish Hamilton

Browne, Anthony (1979) *Bear Hunt.* Hamish Hamilton

Hale, Irina (1982) *Donkey's Dreadful Day.* Macdonald

Hutchins, Pat (1972) *Goodnight Owl.* Picture Puffin

Hutchins, Pat (1976) *Don't Forget the Bacon.* Picture Puffin

Mayer, Mercer (1988) *There's Something Spooky in the Attic.* Macmillan

Nathan and Hedley (1989) *The Cat with Two Tales.* MacDonald

Appendix 2: Story plan copymaster

STORY PLAN

by _____

Who is in your story? How do you introduce them?

Where does it begin? What happens?

What happens next?

How does it end?

Appendix 3: Example of a specific plan

A voyage of exploration

You are composing a letter to the monarch of Spain asking for funding for your voyage of exploration. This drafting chart is to help you decide what to put in your letter. Put down your ideas, and don't be afraid to make changes when you think of better things to put. This is just a rough draft.

> How will you start your letter? (don't forget to say something flattering)

> Draft a sentence or two outlining your plans.

> What are the advantages for Spain?

> List the details you need to include, eg ships, people, length of voyage, etc

> Now make a plea for money - ask for 'funding' or ask for your voyage 'to be sponsored'

> How will you round off your letter?